SHARON L

MIDDLE FINGER HAPPINESS

WORK HARD. LIVE WELL. DON'T F✳CK WITH ME.

i

Cover design by: www.NeueCreative.com [Hector Garcia]
Author photograph: www. martinphoto.co.uk [Brian Martin]
Hair & Makeup: www.shearbeautybylaura.com [Laura Laureles]
Cover Girl: Susan Onstott Graham [Facebook]
Interior design by: www.TheZapataGroup.net
Quotes | Memes: Sharon Lee Zapata

ALSO BY SHARON LEE ZAPATA

The Little Book of Start-Up Inspiration 20 lessons learned the hard way dammit from the most outrageous year of my entrepreneurial life!

It's A New, Day Don't Be A Shit Head

PODCAST: Middle Finger Happiness

WHAT SOME PEOPLE ARE SAYING ABOUT THIS BOOK:

You'll Find Your Bad-assery

"The book shares many instances where the writer had to make serious decisions to be strong. The book is comical, but very moving to someone that has fought similar battles. Make no mistake: if you have underwent any sort of trauma, abuse or neglect, this book has the recipe to overcome and, as the author states #getshitdone. It is a very bold, to the point book of life hacks and reminders that all your battles are there, not to define you, but to prepare you for the person you want to be. Warning: The book may end up making you believe in your own bad-assery, and may potentially ignite and inspire you to get up and tell anyone that is not there to contribute to your journey to eff off!!" ~ MIRZA GARZA

Bold, raw, real and inspirational!

"It's one of those books you pick up and don't want to put down. Author doesn't hold back, in her unique way Sharon shares personal struggles, success and useful information to motivate readers to be the best bad ass version of themselves. I laughed and nodded my head in agreement on many pages! Middle Finger Happiness is the ideal book for anyone at any point in their life. Highly recommend it." ~ANA

WHAT SOME PEOPLE ARE SAYING ABOUT THIS BOOK:

A no frills, no make-up, take no crap, must read!

"Middle Finger Happiness," is chockfull of sage advice from successful life and business survivor; Sharon Lee Zapata, it is a no make-up, no frills, take no crap collection of wise advice for anyone, whether you're already a successful business person or wish to become one. Pulling no punches, her liberal use of the F-Bomb will make you laugh, smile and nod your head in agreement and understanding. I've studied many self-help books by a number of "Professionals," who seem to prescribe and regurgitate the same polished messages "in their own words," of course. (A bit of plagiarism hidden with clever wording.) You will return to this gem again and again, with the understanding that Sharon wants you to be strong-willed and forceful in your endeavors, no matter the challenges! You would be remiss in failing to buy several for family and friends. Once Sharon's valuable insight becomes yours, apply, apply and re-apply the lessons learned!" ~ MANUEL NAVA LEAL, AUTHOR-POET-PLAYWRIGHT

For the Imperfect Person #allofus

"The authenticity of this book is amazing. This book is for the imperfect person, who allows their raw gifts to shine bright like a diamond. Sharon brought tears to my eyes, peace to my soul, and a smile to my face. I loved every minute of it. Cheers to another phenomenal book." ~CRYSTAL

WHAT SOME PEOPLE ARE SAYING ABOUT THIS BOOK:

Love it!

It's not pretty prose. It's real and raw. It's how we think and feel about some of the shitty stuff that happens to us but we're afraid to verbalize. And it's how you get through it. I love Sharon's style of writing because it's just like you're sitting there talking with her. No bs. You're going to love it! ~ C. MEADE, Founder of Nerdy Girls Success

Badass Book

"It's one of those books you pick up and don't want to put down. The author doesn't hold back, in her unique way Sharon shares personal struggles, success and useful information to motivate readers to be the best bad ass version of themselves. I highly recommend this book." ~ VICTORIA PRADO

Entrepreneurs, read this!

Great book for entrepreneurs or anyone who wants to make their ideas happen. 3 pages puts you in monster mode and you just want to get to work, stop caring what society thinks and make your crazy ideas reality. This book definitely competes with best sellers I've seen on the topic. The candid authenticity of the author is gold. ~ JOHN ANTONIO

WHAT SOME PEOPLE ARE SAYING ABOUT THIS BOOK:

Great book and great read!

Love this book! Great read, very motivational and entertaining. While opening herself up, Sharon takes her personal experiences, good and bad, and makes them into a positive thing so that we as readers can get the most out of what she is trying to say and put out there. So happy I read it.

Badass Book

I love this book! I knew I would the second I heard the title. It did not disappoint. It's rare to find a book nowadays that is so beyond honest and still able to make you chuckle. I found this book very insightful. I struggle with depression as well and was hitting rock bottom when this book was given to me. It was just what I needed. I'm team "middle finger happiness" all the way. ~ **Andrew Allen, Author of** The Arrogant Donkey: A Picture Book for Adults

DEDICATION

This book was originally written for me... Not because I have a big ass ego. It's because writing is therapy and it helps to repair the negative shit inside my head.

Then I realized this book is written for you... To remind you how awesome you are no matter how much bull shit you've tolerated or been through.

If you've ever said to yourself, "Fuck it... I am going to make something positive happen for myself!"

Cheers, to your Middle Finger Happiness!

WARNING!

Lots of **"F" bombs** in here motherfuckers... because we're all grown ass women and men and we are products of LIFE.
We have grit and survive with our words, choices, actions, consequences, and results.

We've all come to a crossroad in our lives where we've had to tell a person, a place, or *shituation* to fuck-off...
[no typo: **#shituation** is my new word this year.]

This book is written for those who realize they don't have to wait to ask for permission to improve their lives because insecurity is a fucking liar. This book is ideal for anyone at any point in their life. Whether you feel like you've got your shit together or like it's all falling apart.

You cannot worry what other people are going to think about you when you're attempting to positively re-build the life you want... Not the life *they* want. Don't be surprised if you re-discover your Middle Finger Happiness inside this little book. Let's crack on bitches!

WHAT'S INSIDE?

WHAT'S INSIDE?

SHARON LEE ZAPATA

MIDDLE FINGER HAPPINESS

WORK HARD. LIVE WELL. DON'T FUCK WITH ME.

1st INTRODUCTION

If this book could talk, it would tell you that It's not fucking responsible for what you understand. It's only responsible for being the messenger. The author... well, she's only responsible for her personal, enchanting small batch Middle Finger Happiness stories and the sturdy life lessons she's sharing with you.

Non-risk takers, play-it-safers, people who live without passion, trolls, goblins, and evil narcissist will not understand the significance of Middle Finger Happiness.
They have a middle finger but it's used for picking boogers outta their nose... Just like the **#fucktard** in traffic next to me.

Middle Finger Happiness is a brotherhood and sisterhood that connects us. It's relatable on so many levels. All of us are dealing with some form of bullshit or struggle and we're doing the best to get *un-fucked*. We're durable, original, and slightly irregular. We want to live better lives. Inside this book, we connect-the-dots and uncover how to re-wire our piss poor thinking. We understand that our seemingly wasteful experiences really do push us to understand and accept who we are.

Together, [inside this book] we'll be brave and confidently take our Middle Finger Happiness out of our pockets when life fucks with us. Never lay down from colossal confusion. Listen to your inner voice and take action. This is powerful. This is how to get shit done.

Your inner voice + action = the ingredients to rid *shituations*

Set things straight for yourself because no one else will do this for you sugar lips.

#SECRETTIME NOTE:

Why did Sharon start writing this book? She wants to empower humans who have been made to feel like failures in their attempts to find themselves. She's been there…
How did Sharon start writing this book? She decided to do it. She figured it out. She did it. One Friday afternoon during 5 o'clock fucking traffic, she sat in her over-heated car on a scorching 103° degree day in July in Houston, Texas. While listening to Theory of a Dead man [I Hate My Life] on 94.5 the Buzz radio station, she started thinking about all her successful bad-ass mistakes… she took out her tiny notebook and started writing.
By the way, that song from Theory of a Dead Man is really a happy song…

Don't get too close unless you're comfortable with flaws and torn stitches... Most of us are slightly "irregular"

~ Sharon Lee Zapata

2ND INTRODUCTION

Yes, there is a **2nd introduction** because I am the fucking boss of me... And I felt like doing it.

Here's how I see the world as a writer... content lives all around us. My pen is used freely. I don't think twice. If, I did think twice, nothing would ever be written. (no analysis paralysis) I write every day. I write on great days. I write when I have discouraging days from the outside world. I fucking write without distinguishing features because some days I feel like I'm nobody yet I'm somebody.

I watch and look.
I hear and listen.
I experience life.
I write.

I bang out small batch stories on my sturdy keyboard. Some days I write epic shit. Some days I suck ass and stare at a blank page... and drink another cup of coffee or smoke some weed; because I can. Then I realize if I open up the pain files and the happy files inside my filing-cabinet head without fear; put that story down on paper... then it's naturally released. Yeah, I'm old school bitches... I write with a pen and paper on notebooks and journals. It's at this time of *natural releasing* I've realize who I've grown up to be... A woman with endless possibilities who still struggles because I am only human... Just like you.

I have learned to come to my keyboard with a little knife. I am not afraid to use it. I also write as if nobody is going to fucking read what I write... This is dangerous. This leaves me fearless.

...And maybe a little irresponsible. [insert sinister grin here] I will admit, I am the kind of trouble you would like to be around. When I say *trouble*... I mean I do things that are just on the edge of fascination mixed with responsibilities because I have to get my ass up early in the morning and take my kid to school.

This book was written for two people:

Me and You.

Let's get to know each other inside here. ***It's safe here because it's just us.*** Another reason I wrote this book is because my friend Steve Martinez, [*@CommonSteve* of NeueCreative.com] was one of my first friends to call me and invite me for coffee to *talk* after the release of my 2nd

book.   Steve and I have had a few bad-ass awesome meetings. So, when he calls it's important. He's busy and he always brings laughs, value and influence. Steve "Sharon, I love your new book." *The Little Book of Start-Up Inspiration 20 Lessons Learned the Hard Way Dammit... from the Most Outrageous Year of My Entrepreneurial Life!*
Yeah, that's a long fucking title. It's a keeper!

So, Steve tells me, "Are you working on your next book?"

Me, "No, shit I just published this new book not even a week ago!"

Steve, "Don't wait... get it started. Your readers want to know more about who you are."

Hmmm... I was not sure where to go with this, but I knew I needed to take action. I decided to crack *open* all the files in my head and share...

Life adventures,
Good and bad experiences,
Uncertainty,
Fears, Bravery,
Abuse, Depression

And... Moving on moments, [I call 'em fuck-it moments]
I want to share with you how to hug it out with your fuck-ups.
I want to inspire others so they can embrace their Middle
Finger Happiness too. I also took a few of my most popular
blog posts that were shared at least 100+ times by my
readers. I figured this was good place to start with
copasetic content.

My blog & websites:
 www.TheBitchyBusinessBriefs.com
www.SharonLeeZapata.com
#SharonLeeZapata #TheBitchyBusinessBriefs

CHAPTER

01

If there is no struggle...
there is no progress
If there is no progress...
There is the same shit
from yesterday.

~ Sharon Lee Zapata

NO SELF-HELP STORIES JUST GREAT FUCKING STRUGGLES

Like I mentioned in the beginning of this book, I write for me and for you.

Me: because it helps me straighten out all the shit in my head and in my life. I have depression. It doesn't define me. It's just part of my story. I have learned to smack down my depression with running, cycling, lifting weights, yoga, meditation, and avoiding sugar. I was raised by an abusive narcissist mother and a loving dad who somehow put up with her crazy ass for 25 years. [they've divorced many years ago]. There is no cure for narcissism because there is no cure for evil. I have learned to **#HulkSmash** many problems and move on.

You: because I know there has to be one other person who has gone through the same or similar shituation [no typo] And I guesstimate my writing will help another human being. I don't write self-help books. I write good-struggle books. Most of my small batch story telling I share is about:
how I struggle,
how I've struggled,
and how I will do things to stop struggling.

Life loves to knock us down when we get too tall... and it will show us who we really are. I am quite confident about this topic... I believe I am a *struggling expert*.

"I want to empower humans who have been made to feel like failures in their attempts to find themselves."
Sharon Lee Zapata

**You can strut standing still...
Don't' weigh yourself
with pounds.
Weigh yourself with
achievements and successful
mistakes.**

~ Sharon Lee Zapata

I am dyslexic. I am bi-lingual. I am spicy. I am mild.

I am kind. I am a hard-ass.

I am self-aware and sometimes I don't give a shit.

I wonder about stuff and I wander too.

I have confidence in some areas and I lack confidence in other areas.

Some of my struggles are unheard-of.

Unheard-of is a good story.

I type my little stories on my keyboard...

It sounds like I'm pissed-off as I type quickly on the keys of my mini iPad, but I'm not pissed-off.

I am excited as I write this book!...

I sound like I'm super busy in this coffee shop.

And I move on...

I write about the hot Texas Summertime in the late 70's when I got drop off by myself at the public pool in elementary school. Imagine me at Age-10 a very petite girl in my bright yellow swimsuit purchased from a grocery store. [yeah, my mother stopped into a grocery store to get me a 'swimsuit'… because that's where people go to buy swimsuits?]
I think about the time when kids photo's would show up on milk cartons. Some of you may be too young to remember this. I never understood why *milk cartons* where picked as the marketing platform to put missing kids photos on.

Missing kids photos should've been on beer cans too. You know why? Because my drunk-ass uncle would send me and my cousin to the Seven-11 convenient corner store to buy his beer and cigarettes for him. We could have easily *disappeared* but we didn't.

So, yeah leaving your petite 10-year old girl alone at the public pool was unheard-of... because nowadays kids go missing in situations like this. I was small for my age... And I was struggling to keep my confidence up as I was looking around the public neighborhood pool for my cousins who were supposed to be there...

I write about the old ass lady with her hot pink swimming cap that snuggly hugged her Q-tip shaped head as she swam laps in the pool that summer. Her words vaulted out of her mouth... as she told me to jump in the deep end of the pool dammit!

"Be afraid and do it anyway kid!" she shouted at me with a rebel cry and her defiant fist in the air as she saw me staring down at the water looking dazed and confused.

This is just one of my unheard-of hotter than hell Texas Summer stories. I learned that I have to be afraid and do things anyway.

I jumped into deep end of the swimming pool thinking I was going to die. I did not die. I learned that my struggle was just fear. It changed me forever.

Fear is just a feeling.
Fear can create unheard-of struggles.
It can fuck with our heads.
Have you ever been afraid?
I've been afraid.

When I wrote my first book in 2004 *"The 12 Secrets for Successful Hispanic Women"* I was going through a personal struggle and once again... I was afraid to write. *[P.S. I wouldn't buy that book. It's boring. It's generic. I wasn't writing in my true fucking authentic voice like I write now.]* I was struggling with the negative seasonal relationship I had with my abusive narcissist mother at that time. Narcissists are hard to deal with because they are never willing to recognize that something is wrong with them and they need no help. There is no cure for narcissism because there is no cure for evil. I have learned to detach myself from attachment-drama. **#PeaceOut**

"The rolla-costa-twista...

Suppose-ta love ya narcissista-momma, even though I'm not supposed ta. She's cruel. You've gone too far... who do you think you are?"

~ S. L. Zapata

Narcissist are awesome at making you feel like *you're the one* who is fucked up. They lie to everyone and everyone believes them.

#SECRETTIME NOTE: I have been journaling and writing for over 20 years... I have tons of notebooks in my home-office with stories of struggles, happiness, good times, bad times, heart breaks, first kiss, last kiss, moving on moments, and so much more... They say it takes 10,000 hours of doing something to become an expert... I've been writing for more than 10,000 hours, but it doesn't make me an expert. It just makes me an *open book* of curiosities for my readers.

As a lonely teenager whose dad was in the military, we traveled a lot and I found myself writing daily in my little spiral notebooks and journals. I attended (8) eight different schools in (12) twelve years. I passionately thought about becoming a writer. My narcissist mother told me that writing *was not a real* job. At 16-years old, hearing this just solidified that I would never become a writer.

"When you're young fear is how you fall."
~Sharon Lee Zapata

This was just the beginning of a Middle Finger Happiness moment that would circle back around in my life. You know what's even crazier? The same week my *mother told me that* being a writer was not a real job I was offered an amazing opportunity at only 16 years old. My English high school teacher loved my short stories and offered me a journalist internship at the *ABC-television station KATU in Portland, Oregon.*

I was a sophomore attending Centennial High School in Gresham, Oregon. I never forgot how happy it made me that someone believed in my writing at 16-years old.   I did not get to participate in that internship opportunity. We moved back to Corpus Christi, Texas [this sucked ass].

My heart was broken, however, it didn't stop me from continuing to write in my little spiral notebooks and journals. Writing was my therapist.

It's always the mutha-fuckas with no magic telling you what do do with your magic...

~ Sharon Lee Zapata

I was not aware of it at the time, but writing is **_actual therapy_** and it's one of the best tools for **_self-exploration_**. Writing also challenges your capacity for understanding your personal world. Writing is your ability to demonstrate logic and showcase your verbal dexterity to help others.

Laa-dee-daa muthafuckas! Fast forward today... I am riding my wave! Cheers to my **#MiddleFingerHappiness**

I am the author of {3} new books, an entrepreneur, podcaster, business owner, writer/blogger, artist, philanthropist, and mom of two awesome boys.
I speak to audiences about finding their passion and their Middle Finger Happiness. Some days I am insecure, but I push myself because I know there are many levels to help other people... but first I help myself. **#PushYourself**
#GetYourShitTogether

CHAPTER

02

It takes fucking courage to grow up and turn out to be who you really are.

– Sharon Lee Zapata

IT TAKES FUCKING COURAGE TO GROW UP AND BE YOU

[Especially if you've experience abuse]

In 2004 I was apprehensive about writing my very first book. I had the support of my awesome man, Felipe Zapata. He kept nudging me to just do it. After he read my hidden journals and notebooks, he became instrumental in putting things into direction to get that book published. Here we are in 2019 and technology makes it so easy now to write and publish a book.

Do you remember the story of the old ass lady with the hot pink swimming cap and the Q-tip shaped head? *(Chapter 1)* With her rebel shout at the public swimming pool she told me to jump in! *"Be afraid and do it anyway"*

Fuck it. I wrote that little book even with the fear I had inside my head. I took action and didn't stop until my book was done. **#Boom #Bam #Bitch.**

In 2004, I wrote *12 Secrets For Successful Hispanic Women.* It wasn't because I was trying to teach Hispanic women about *secrets* to be successful... I wrote it because I was lacking self confidence in some areas of my life yet I had high self confidence when it came to *not giving up...*

I know this doesn't make sense. It is what it is. So, I shared all the *secrets* I knew at that time about *"**how not to give up**"*. That book was in Barnes & Noble, Borders book stores… you know… traditional book signings.

I had the honor of being a guest speaker for The South-Texas Hispanic Women's Conference at the University of Houston [Victoria, TX] campus. I shared the stage with actress and activist Jackie Guerra. Some of you might remember her from the movie *Selena*. Jackie had the role of the drummer in the movie.

I felt so proud of myself because that afternoon I not only inspired 400 women in the audience, in 30-minutes I also earned $4,000 in books sales and an amazing speaker's fee [for me at that time]. It made my heart smile to have women come up to me with tears in their eyes and say how inspired they were… and how they too were ready to make positive changes in their lives. When I returned home after that amazing conference, I had a shitty conversation with my narcissist mother… She had the nerve to tell me, "You call that a book?"

"Fuck you", is what I should have told her… but I didn't. I was frozen in disbelief. A slide show of painful images flickered through my mind... Oh shit, I had flash-backs of all her negative conversations; especially the conversation when she told me that being a writer was not a real job.

She was just pissed off because inside that book I mentioned how my parents were unhappily married for years. I guess she didn't want anybody knowing this. But I got news for her... everybody knew. **#SecretTimeBitch**

That remark stifled my creativity and made me want to crawl away from my passion of writing... Fuck me, I should have not listened to her. I share this with you just in case you've been told something to crush your spirit.

Now, if I had received positive constructive criticism on my writing that's a different story. C'mon, if I suck at something I am alright hearing about it. But, if I don't suck and you just want to piss on my rainbow because you have more issues than Vogue Magazine, then that's when I whip out my Middle Finger Happiness to remind myself that I'm my own little super-hero. **#NoTimeForBullshit**.

That conversation with her really crushed my heart and fucked with my head so bad. I stopped believing in myself for about three years. I also fell into deep depression. Some of you may be thinking... really?! That statement made you go into depression? Well, motherfuckers what you don't know is how I carried the traumatized recollection from her physical abuse as a little kid… and verbal abuse [well into adulthood].

One of many fucked up stories that I'll share with you… Is when I was 5-years old in kindergarten, I threw up one morning at the breakfast table. My mother stood over me and slammed my head on the kitchen table. She made me scoop up my vomit and eat it. Then I was tossed like a rag doll into my room where I fell down on my face and hit the sharp metal corner rail of my twin-sized bed. I was so shaken up. Trembling, I quietly walked into the bathroom to clean myself up. I was traumatized going to school that morning. How could she do this to me? I was small and helpless. I was confused and torn inside because I always thought our parents are supposed to love us and protect us… not harm us.

 I walked into my kindergarten class room with a bloody nose; my teacher asked me what happened to my face? I told her that I fell.   That morning was also class picture day. I remember sitting on the front row of the group classroom picture with my hands folded on my lap. The photographer kept asking me to smile… and I just couldn't. He had no idea how my morning had started… I still have a scar under my nose from that horrific incident. As I write this, I still have mixed emotions. I am pissed off. I am also strong and say fuck her.

I threw up a lot during Kindergarten through 2nd grade [especially mornings before school]. I recall going to the doctor and having x-rays done of my stomach. The doctors could not figure out what was wrong with me. Looking back now as an adult, I know that vomiting can be a common symptom of anxiety and stress. Stress was fucking unbelievable in our home. My parents yelling at each other, my dad drinking, and my mom's abuse. That's the landscape I recall as a little kid. Many Friday nights I would pack up little suit case with my coloring books, crayons, and my stuff animals.

Friday night was the beginning of the weekend and I wanted to run away from my home. Since I was only 5 or 6 years old I couldn't drive a fucking car, so I would just sit outside under the stairwell of our apartment.... Staring at the stars, crying and daydreaming; wishing I could go somewhere better.

But I couldn't... I was just a little kid.
By the time I was in 2nd or 3rd grade the physical abuse from my mother stopped and I became a really quiet kid.

However, the verbal abuse continue for years... Because that's what narcissist do.

Everyone would always say, "She's so quiet and smart..."
If they only knew, there was a Kraken inside that petite quiet girl. *[Chapter 3, I talk more about the fucking Kraken!]*

One summer, I started talking to my cousins about my home life. Nobody really believed me. I have always tolerated a tumultuous relationship with my narcissist mother. This is the fucking rollercoaster of being raised by a narcissist. My parents finally divorced after 25-years of marriage. I have a great relationship with my dad. He is unbelievably supportive. He doesn't drink. We have deep conversations now about life and we laugh. Thanks dad, I love you.

I've attempted so many times to work things out with her, however, it's beyond repair. It's FUBAR [fucked-up beyond all repair]. I no longer speak with my narcissist mother... and most likely never will. *[Chapter 4 It's Alright to Tell a Narcissist to Fuck Off]*

Refusing to apologize is not a sign of strength. It's a sign of narcissism.

~ Sharon Lee Zapata

Fast forward… the unstoppable support from my dad, my husband, my brother, friends, research, therapy and reading books... I've re-built myself [and continue to do so.]

Occasionally, I still have small flashback moments of her negative words. The mind can be a battle-field. We win in this battle by taking control of our thoughts… not by letting our thoughts control us. When this happens, I stop and take a deep breath and remember all the amazing shit I have accomplished in my life.

The beautiful successful mistakes that have brought me to this very moment of writing this page for us to share. If I hadn't eaten some shit-sandwiches in my life… I wouldn't be who I am now. I use the metaphor of 'shit-sandwiches' for all the bullshit I've been through. I am sure you can relate…

I wouldn't be the writer I am now. I would not be able to help other people who've also been through times of fuckery. I've learned that depression can stem from being raised by a parent or parents who are narcissist. This is a "No-Shit-Sherlock" moment… when I was researching my depression.

#SECRETTIME NOTE:

This is the 3rd book I write. My desire is for *this book* to help someone else who has been through similar *shituations*. You would think that I know what I am doing with all this writing. It's something I've had to learn and re-learn and keep learning. Because I put so much of *who I am* when I write; it feels like I bleed on the keyboard sometimes writing about bad memories, personal struggles, and the worm-hole of my life lessons.

It requires something else from me… something more each time I write a new book. I still feel like an amateur. I am still learning how to do this. Even Hemingway once said, *"We are all apprentices in a craft no one ever masters."*

I still grip words with passion so I can diligently share what I used to be afraid of. Can you believe I used to be afraid to write? Fuck that. It's the stories we're most embarrassed about that people want to connect with. The human landscape is connected with: thoughts, words, actions, and inactions.

Story-telling is how we learn and how we connect.

By sharing my writing, my blog and social media platforms, I have organically grown an amazing large audience of dedicated readers and followers. Thank you for your continued support.

I built this with bravery.

You will love *Chapter 15 Bravery Lives Inside Dark Cracks.* Every time I finish writing... I hit enter and send.

I don't look back. I still write like nobody is going to read what I post...

This is the awkward freedom I give myself.
So, far so good.
I am and always will be under construction ...

Brave [breyv]

adjective, **brav·er, brav·est.**
possessing or exhibiting courage or courageous
endurance.

NOTE TIME:

List 1 time you had to be brave?

_____

_____

_____

How did it make you feel?

_____

_____

_____

Were you born to resist or be abused? I swear I'll never give in... I refuse.

- Dave Grohl, Foo Fighters

CHAPTER

03

What is Middle Finger Happiness?
It's whatever the fuck you want it
to be...
As long as it creates a better
quality of life and positive growth.

~ Sharon Lee Zapata

WHAT IS MIDDLE FINGER HAPPINESS?

If you've ever said to yourself, *"Fuck it... I am going to go make something positive happen for myself because I've wanted to for a long time!"*

Or you've just gotten to a point in
your life, in your career,
in your relationship(s)
Where you know that you have to change...
for the better – for the positive.

Even, if it means upsetting everything and everyone around you. ...And even if it means breaking your own heart.
This is *#MiddleFingerHappiness* dammit. I came up with the hash-tag **(#middlefingerhappiness)** during the Thanksgiving - Christmas holidays... November - December of 2017.

Go figure... it was the jolly, jolly, fucking holidays. {If you're new to my writing... this is how I roll with a beautiful potty-mouth} Don't get me wrong, I do enjoy the holidays with special friends and family. If you really want to know?... My favorite holiday is Halloween! It's dark, yet happy with pumpkin spice paraphernalia everywhere!

So, where was I? Oh, yeah the holidays! That special time of the year when we can get an aggressive fingering in our check-book [metaphorically speaking] with shopping, driving around in crazy traffic, attending parties, get-togethers, and our pocketbooks get emptied out faster than an overstuffed elevator with someone's stink-bomb fart.

Money can be tight and the holidays can be very stressful... like that ball of tangled up Christmas Tree Lights you have to un-do every year. Depression can kick in too during this merry time of the year. I have depression. It does not identify me. It's just part of my story. I don't use it as an excuse not to live my life to its fullest. We all have an invisible expiration date stamped on us... just like on that gallon of 2% milk in your refrigerator.

I'm a realist. Can you tell? So, I figured out that the faster I smack down my depression, the better for me and those around me. I have learned to smash the shit out of my depression through [an active lifestyle] running, cycling, lifting weights, meditation, yoga and avoiding sugar.

Because I share tons of free content on social media and on my blog, I would write the hash-tag [*#middlefingerhappiness*] at the end of my posts. It has gone viral. Just type in #middlefingerhappiness in a browser bar and see what happens... Shit, I think someone created a website in Greek with all my quotes. I heard somewhere: **People will take from you what they can't create themselves.**

#MiddleFingerHappiness is something so simple that many people can identify with... Everyone has some Middle Finger Happiness in their soul. One of my favorite tattoos I have is on my arm that reads:

Middle Finger Happiness

Thank you, B.K. and Allen from Prison Break Tattoos in Houston, TX. Look these guys up if you need an awesome creative ink! They are known for doing all the tattoos for the brave Houston Policemen and Houston Firemen.

How do you get to point in your life where you want Middle Finger Happiness? The answer is not easy... and it's different for everyone. It is not easy to get *#MiddleFingerHappiness* especially if it includes other people's hearts and they have attached their heart-strings to you. Like I said earlier, I wrote this book for me and for you. It's your little hand-book with real-life saucy advice, inspirational smart-ass quotes, twisted humor... a lot of F bombs, and so much more. I want to help you create the courage to wipe-out the very thing that holds you back from moving forward.

Or, maybe it's just a cool little book you picked up because of the catchy title and you had no fucking clue what it's all about... and you've made it this far into my book.

Congrats! You're here... Keep reading! You're on this joy ride now! I'm not writing as an expert... just as a person who's on a journey. I'm a person who's been through a lot of stumbling and getting up... How about you?
I am a person who doesn't give up when pursuing something I want to accomplish. How about you?

I wasn't always like this. I wasn't always the type of person who doesn't give up. Growing up I was a quiet and insecure kid. Most likely due to the physical and verbal abuse I received from my narcissist mother. I used to be unsure about myself and I would worry what other people would think of me if I released the fucking Kraken that I really am.

SPECIAL NOTE: For some of you bitches who don't know what the Kraken is... THE Kraken is a monster in the movie "Clash of the Titans." Zeus, king of the gods, barks the order to, **"Release the Kraken!"** He shouts this line in the movie, it's a huge, monstrous beast, a bit like an over sized octopus on steroids, and it quickly became a cult favorite. Technically, it means **"Release the monster"** It's a phrase for letting all hell break loose.

I am constantly in my own head just like the rest of you who are reading this... When we blatantly share our secrets and unsavory stories by opening our closet of bones and allow those bones to fall out into a little pile... we discover personal healing. This healing can also be *Middle Finger Happiness*. As a writer, my healing is done with a keyboard and words. I do this best when I am transparent and share with my readers.

The whole point to this little book is so we can learn how to confidently navigate on our personal journeys with open arms... not folded arms. Open spaces await you!
But you won't see those open spaces with depression and your head down... or with your head stuck up your ass.

Don't ask me where I heard that *head stuck up your ass* line... I think it's a Texas saying... not sure, but I like it.

Let's crack on to the next chapter.
This one is over now... turn the page

CHAPTER 04

Your hugs feel like
'fuck You'
This is how a narcissist
gives hugs...

#NoEasyCome #NoEasyGo #JustGoBitch

- Sharon Lee Zapata

IT'S ALRIGHT TO TELL A NARCISSIST TO FUCK OFF

Earth to Sharon... yep that's what I tell myself once in a while when I space out and replay hurtful conversations inside my head. We all do it no matter how positive we want to be... this shit enters our minds. It's like we all have a tiny fink in our head who likes to occasionally appear and point out negative things...

You've done it.
I've done it.
We've done it.

Shit, you're probably gonna do it sometime today... Don't worry, after reading this, you'll become more impervious to negative self-talk. I will share with you how to unravel or how to become more free from difficult, un-repairable situations... especially situations with a narcissist.

I believe you'll have a better grip on what to tell yourself so you can repair the *shoulda-coulda-woulda* moments in your world.
I am an avid reader.
I am a book worm.
I read three (3) to six (6) books a month.

I read non-fiction and a little fiction.

I've read my fair share of *self-improvement books, forgive people books, meditation books, empower yourself books,* articles, and research topics. Why these topics? Because of my up-bring... that's why.

I say *forgive...* just *don't* forget.

I also say don't forgive... and tell someone to fuck off.

If you don't agree with me... no worries.

I am not writing to get people to *agree* with me.

I am writing my book with my calculations, experiences, and how I've chipped away at problems and nasty people. [*fucktards* is a better word for them]

The way we understand and perceive our *individual* worlds will vary. We are not all the same... but what helps us to connect-the-dots as humans, are the stories we share.

You see, the hard stuff we go through should never be forgotten. It should be used to thicken our armor so we can take on life's next battle we encounter. Do not be a door mat when someone fucks with you or your loved ones. No matter how positive and sunny we want to look at life... a crappy shituation will pop up around and pounce on us. I am not being negative. I am a realist. I have a soft, mushy loveable heart. Like a giant strawberry flavored gummy bear. It's there for the people in my life that I truly love. The people who set my heart on fire. I will fight like a motherfucker to protect them too. I also have a hardened-heart. The heart that's been ripped through my asshole... it has pieces of shard glass; it sits on bar stool in the corner with a pair of dark sunglasses, a tequila shot and a cigarette. **#DoNotFuckWithMe.**

Why? Why... would I do this? Aren't we supposed to forgive others who have harmed us? Yes, however, we are also supposed to be emotionally strong enough to take on whatever life deals us. When you have a hardened heart and a soft heart, you know which heart to fight with and to love with...

They say we need patience. Yes we do need patience for certain things. [not sure who *They* are...] probably some greasy hair guy named Beauregard who sits in a dark room with multiple telephones all labeled "*They*."

Then there are times when patience has to take a fucking backseat because impatience gets shit done. This is reality. In my 40's I finally reached a point in my life when I stopped talking to my narcissist mother. My mother is a fucking piece of work. To this day, I probably still have family members who would not believe some of the crazy shit she has said and done to me. *They* don't live my life. I don't have time to gather all the people around to explain... and neither do you if you have a similar *shituation*.

Our personal clocks are ticking every day to live.

To create.

To produce.

To eliminate.

To re-create.

To be a great moms and/or dads

And most importantly... to be the best people we can be

And to look in the mirror without regrets.

There is freedom when we're truly ready to tell someone to fuck off. They really have had to earned that... like an Olympic medalist for evil shit-heads... You know exactly what I am talking about. Pioneering risk-taking decisions take openness to stand up for yourself. Nobody can see what's inside your delicate yet fucking strong mind. Everything is a choice. Not choosing is a choice.

Permanently detaching from a toxic, hurtful relationship(s) is better than 'tolerating'. I know this from personal experience. Cutting off my relationship with my narcissist abusive mother is one of the hardest yet best choices I've ever had to do. Narcissists cannot change [there is no cure for evil] - - so the best thing to do is to leave and protect yourself. I know some family members aren't going to understand this. That's not my problem. Narcissist always have a "favorite" or "golden" child in their family. Narcissist also have a "scapegoat" child. In other words, one child is perfect and capable of doing no wrong. The other child is seen as the black sheep, and the cause of all issues.

I was the 'winner-winner-chicken-dinner' Ha! Ha! I was the 'scapegoat' child! Fucking awesome to be this! Why? Why? Why? Would I say this?

I say it with my Middle Finger Happiness because I wouldn't be writing this chapter. Learning how to understand and make peace with your childhood is one of the most healing and empowering experiences you could ever go through.

The decision for a permanent division is pure freedom.
People with freedom are stronger.
People who are stronger can help themselves.
People who are stronger can help others.

Part of being a strong person, is knowing when to put yourself first and when to look out for others. Not everyone will agree that it's alright to tell someone to fuck off. They can go write their own book about this.

Dammit, if someone had shared with me how they've

moved on and re-built themselves because of similar experiences and *shituations*; I would've been open to listening to them. Most likely it would have saved me years of heart-ache, confusion, and feeling worthless. Well, here I am today sharing my experience(s) and telling you how I've dealt with fuck 'em moments in my life... and how I've moved on. **#MovingOnMoments**

There will be people who pick up this book... because the title caught their eye. However, if they're easily offended, they'll shake their heads because they don't *'get-it'*. That's alright. I'm not writing for them. I am writing for you and me.

I do not write self-help books.
I write good-struggle books and how to do things to stop struggling. I don't sell books. I take you on a personal empowerment magic carpet ride with a sturdy, torn carpet. Together we'll grip hands as we dive down and swoop up and over our stains of time. Sorta like a drone that can see ass-clowns and obstacles from above...

CHAPTER 05

Plowing through the shit
you're going through ...
is preparing you to kickass
#workhard
#livewell
#dontfuckwithme

- Sharon Lee Zapata

WHAT STRONG WOMEN & MEN DON'T GIVE A FUCK ABOUT

1.] They don't give a fuck or worry about what other people think about them.

Being yourself means doing *it* no matter what people think. Some people will always try to bring you down and tear you apart, and it's up to you to have thick skin [like a rhinoceros] enough to shrug it off. By the same token, though, it's important to listen to constructive criticism and to work on improving yourself. Learn how to take on honest advice from well-meaning people and when to ignore assholes, fuck-nuggets, and toxic people who only want to push you down the worm-hole.

2.] They know they don't need to be nice all the time.

Being nice is great until you come face to face with someone [a fucktard] who couldn't care less about being nice. Then you need to be mean. 'Speak softly and carry a big stick'. Always be ready to stand up for and to protect yourself when necessary.

3.] They aren't fucking afraid to be themselves.

A life lived being anything other than your true self is a life not truly lived. You have to be true to yourself. Be you and no one else, and the best possible version of yourself, at that.

CHAPTER 06

If you spend your life pretending to be someone else, you waste the person you are...

#DontFukcingWasteWhoYouAre

- Sharon Lee Zapata

WHAT STRONG WOMEN & MEN DO GIVE A FUCK ABOUT

1.] They take responsibilities for their choices and decisions.

This life is on you. It isn't the result of anything other than your own choices and actions. Strong women and men don't blame other people or systems for their lack of anything. This is worthy of repeating. *Stop blaming others for your lack of anything. Start taking control of your life, your thoughts, and your choices or just shut the fuck up.*

2.] They keep pushing forward to a better functioning position.

Look... life can suck. It can be harsh. We've seen bad shit happen to good people. Strong women and men [mentally strong] make tough choices to look at the bright side of situations. They have trained their thinking to appreciate and look for the good in their lives... even when life sucks. They don't shy away from change. Making changes can be uncomfortable. The world revolves around change.

Seasons change –

There is night and day –

People are born –

People die... change is never ending.

We've all heard how we need to get out of our comfort zones. When we shy away from change, it prevents us from growing into the badass persons we were meant to be. The longer we wait to change the harder it gets. And... other people will out-grow you.

3.] They observe other strong women and men.

Strong women and men look up to each other as role models and sources of inspiration. They are generous with their recognition and view others that they see as strong, and they are able to draw strength through their admiration.

CHAPTER 07

Don't adjust to other's offenses... Be so focused and occupied on your own shit and your own progress that you could care less or not at all...

#MiddleFingerHappiness

- Sharon Lee Zapata

FIND YOUR STRONG
(What Are You Badass At?)

Being an authentic individual is the best thing you can do for you and for others. There's enough hard work for your body and mind to not be who really are. **#YouBeYou**

People always appreciate honesty over 'fake-ass-fucks' Yeah, you've thought about this too. Let me unpack some real talk here... Growing up my teachers would tell me to focus and improve on my weaknesses. In high school I struggled horribly with Algebra. I failed Algebra three [3] years in a row... WTF? (what the fuck?) Yes. **#ThisIsMe**

Add this *failure* to a young girl who already struggled with self-esteem issues. Great recipe for "You'll never amount to shit." I had horrible self-talk with myself when I was young.
Finally, I made a C- grade in Algebra and passed! Crazy... I sat in the same damn room and the same damn desk every year. I had the same teacher every year too. His name was Mr. Aguirre. Looking back, he was a quiet and patient teacher. His calmness almost made him seem like he was stoned... I liked his class because I liked him. I still didn't like Algebra.

First find an equation of variation.

C = kS

67.5 = k x 6 substituting 75 for C and 6 for S

67.5= k

6

11.25 =k

The equation of variation is C = 11.25 S

(WTF?) What the fuck?

I've never, never had to use this in my life...

Again, I did not like Algebra.

I liked looking out the window at the trees; listening to the birds... and writing in my journal.

No matter if you're young or old...
When life puts you through a challenge, you'll learn what you're awesome at

~ Sharon Lee Zapata

In school I excelled in writing, art, language, and history. Fast forward, I ran into Mr. Aguirre about 15 years after I graduated from high school. I was in the grocery store buying eggs. I passed him in the isle... and then I remembered! My old high school teacher! [who always seemed to be stoned...]

"Wow! What are you doing?!" he asked!

"I'm not doing Algebra!", I said!

"How are you ?!", he asked.

Me, "Unbelievable!"

Side note: If I ever meet you and say, "I'm unbelievable..." it's because I have way too much shit to share with you and I want to keep it light, tight, and short. Just saying.

He asked me what I was up to? And I let him know I became an entrepreneur, business owner, artist, writer, and author.

Guess what he says next? Yes! I always knew you were going to write or do something creative like that. It was at that very moment I realized how we shouldn't waste time and waste years struggling to find 'our strong' [the thing(s) that we're naturally badass at]...

Don't focus your time and energy on something you're not great at. It's a waste of your limited time. We were all born with factory-installed gifts and talents. The world doesn't reward mediocrity.

"You can strut standing still… don't weigh yourself with pounds. Weigh yourself with achievements and successful mistakes."
~ Sharon Lee Zapata

When was the last time you looked at what comes naturally to you? That is where you should go. Polish those natural skill(s) and get them shiny as fuck! **#MiddleFingerHappiness**

Now, I understand we all have jobs that pay bills. We have responsibilities. We cannot just get up and go and leave our J.O.B. [just over broke]. Maybe some of you reading this book can do this. However, the majority of people cannot. I know this from personal experience.

Shit, one of my first jobs in my early twenties… I unloaded trucks for an Arts and Craft store in Corpus Christi, TX. It sucked ass. It was hot outdoor laborious work. Unloading trucks was not my bad-ass skill… however, it did pay the bills at that time. At 5'3" 120 lbs. it was hard for me to do the work. But I did it. I was sharing a house with room-mates and I had bills and of course I wanted to go to happy hour with the girls... Dumb shit we do in our 20's! The older I got, the more I started looking at how my life was heading. I wasn't satisfied. I went back to college.

To make this chapter short... let's just say, it took me 10 years, owning and selling several businesses, and two failed marriages to get my Associates Degree in Liberal Arts.

I finally went on to the University of Houston Downtown... to get my B.A. in Communications. I laugh, because I *almost* finished college. If you know me personally, I am known for finishing what I start 90% of the time. **#GetShitDone**.

I take my goals and projects very seriously. However, I will happily share with you that without my *completed* 4-year degree, I have built several successful businesses and sold them... today I am a proud college dropout. Yes, I am just shy of a few college courses to get my B.A. Communications degree.

Yet, I am the CEO [Chief Energy Officer] of my own company, a speaker, a mentor, the author of several books, and I've teamed up with other entrepreneurs and non-profits to feed the homeless in Houston, TX **#WeFeedHTX**.

I've worked diligently on annual back to school 'BACKPACK' campaigns with IKSH [I Know Somebody Houston], as well as campaigns with The Texas Alliance of Military Women Leadership Circle to help veterans here in my city of Houston, Texas. I am also the mom of two amazing boys who I love dearly. I consider myself very successful without my degree.

Sometimes you just have to say, "Fuck it; I want to do something bigger and better with my life." This is definitely one way to grab hold of your personal Middle Finger Happiness.

It could be starting your own company, leaving a bad relationship(s), moving to a new city, and just taking action on what you want. I've done all the above!
Become impervious [unmoved] by negative comments:

"You're too young!"
"You're too old!"
"That won't work"
"You have no money to start that"
"That's never going to work"

...These are untrue LIES people say to others...don't ever let an asshole steal your dreams **#MiddleFingerHappiness**

No lame excuses to make something happen for yourself.

Find your *'strong'*.

You want something you've never had?...

You have to do something you've never done...

We all have an invisible expiration date stamped on us...

Live your life to your fucking fullest potential before you die.

CHAPTER 08

Avoid unchallengingly occupations... They will waste your talents and your natural genius flair!

~ Sharon Lee Zapata

16 Questions to Ask Yourself When You Are Re-inventing Yourself

[1.] Was I always like this?

[2.] Why didn't I see this shit coming?

[3.] Does everyone go through this?

[4.] How long will this fucking last?

[5.] How long will this fucking matter?

[6.] What if I realize it isn't me? ...It's you!

[7.] What if I don't want to take one for the team because the team sucks!

[8.] Are my battle-tested experiences enough to take on this new thing?

[9.] Is my lack of physical fitness stopping me from following my dreams?

[10.] What is the outcome of having a relationship with me?

[11.] How do I connect with influencers and what value do I bring?

[12.] What if the point is... That there is no point?

[13.] What is the best advice I can give myself today?

[14.] What people, places and things are cluttering up my life?

[15.] Where do I want to be 5 years from now?

[16.] Is it me... or is it hot in here?

CHAPTER 09

Life is going to get hard sometimes. Get the fuck up and get your shit together. You're either an ocean or a puddle. People walk through puddles like they're nothing. Oceans Fucking destroy cities

~ Andy Frisella, MFCEO Podcast

Do This... When Life is Fucking with You

We've all had really bad things happens to us. Nobody is immune to not living a problem free life. Fault and responsibility are two very different things... Yet they go hand in hand when life is fucking around with us. As I write this chapter, I am going through something personal and extremely hard. Even with all the struggles I have smacked down in my life... this particular problem seems like a tsunami covering me. I am indirectly involved because it is a shituation [no typo] that my oldest son is going through.

As a mom, it's hard to see him go through his situation. I am savvy enough to know that it is his battle to fight. Even with all the family support, he still has to make tough decisions and take pro-active actions. Daily, many people are accused of things they did not do. Because of legal reasons, I cannot discuss or write about the details of this *shituation*. As parents of grown children it's still hard to see them go through a horrible ordeal. He has seen me be strong and fight during my life [divorce, single mom, dealing with my narcissist mother, yaddy, yaddy, yaddy...] He has also seen how a great marriage is supposed to work... Yeah, it takes fucking work to have an awesome marriage. Thank you to Felipe Zapata for being an unbelievable strong, loving stepdad and husband. My son is aware that my sturdy and durable positive influence has always been here for him. I'm not telling you this so you can feel sorry for me. You have enough of your own personal shit to deal with. I simply want you to benefit positively from what I am writing. Writing is therapy. Writing is how I inspire myself and others...

My personal Middle Finger Happiness philosophy
decisions + actions = results.

Sounds pretty simple.

And sometimes it is...

And sometimes it's the hardest shit we'll ever do...

Solving painful problems doesn't define us.

Solving painful problems is part of our story.

What's really fucked up is when we did nothing to get emotionally caught up in a hurtful situation... where we had no control.

The majority of us are broken humans *working*. Yes, with cracks, chips, and worn out shields we keep fighting

 So what do I suggest when life is fucking with you?

My 5 Personal Dirty Secrets When Life is Fucking with You:

[1.] Acknowledge that all your life you will have some sort of problem(s)

[2.] Dealing with our personal reality is always the answer. Expectations are never the answer.

[3.] The faster you make a strong decision and the faster you take action the quicker you can go on to the next smack-down. Plus your confidence builds every time you do this.

[4.] Strengthen or enhance the lives of others with your experience... In other words, share the good stuff you know that will help them.

[5.] Reclaim your confidence no matter how hard it is... with the lump in your throat, with your racing heart-beat, with tears rolling down your face. Fuck it. Be brave. Get your #MiddleFingerHappiness outta your pocket and never put it back!

Most humans will continue to think about their the past...
You know the shoulda, coulda, woulda... Because that's the
AVERAGE mental landscape that most humans create for
themselves.

Some people will continue to get lost inside their own minds
thinking they are insignificant, invaluable, and that there is
no way out of their bad situation. But we are not AVERAGE!
Come on... anybody who picks up this book title: Middle
Finger Happiness [Work hard. Live well. Don't Fuck With Me.]
- - is not an AVERAGE person.

Remember if you want to help an adult get over a shitty
problem, you can only *influence* them. You *cannot control*
them. You can suggest. In the end, it will be up to them to
fight their own battles. So, why do some people conquer
problems faster and better than others? According to Dr.
Joe Dispenza, author of *Becoming Supernatural – How
Common People Are Doing the Uncommon*, they do this
because they have conditioned themselves to think
differently. Go back to #3 on My 5 Personal Dirty Secrets
When Life is Fucking with You.

Did you know we can re-wire our neurons in our brains?

Neurons: *The neuron is the basic working unit of the brain, a specialized cell designed to transmit information to other nerve cells and muscles. [like super highway]*

Thoughts are actually programs to our brains, however, the emotions we have connected to those thoughts are what control our actions. We can learn and change in a state of suffering or we can learn and change in a state of joy and inspiration. Shit, I say learn joy and inspiration… suffering sucks. **#BeenThereDoneThat**

Some people wait until they're in a really shitty situation in order to change. Why wait? Change now to make a better life. How you think and how you feel creates your state of *being.* If you're constantly thinking about a past fucking negative event… you'll never be able to live in the present and create the life you were meant to live.   Re-read that last sentence - - is says; if you're **constantly** thinking about a past fucking negative event…

Yes, negative events can be like finks that pop into our heads. We need to invite them to leave. Emotions are the end products of past experiences. Also, being physically fit and having the strongest body possible actually controls your brain. The body is stronger than the mind when it is 'exercised'. I mentioned in an earlier chapter how I have smacked-down my depression by running, lifting weights, yoga, cycling and avoiding sugar. I have basically repaired myself physically and emotionally from the abuse of being raised by a narcissist mother. *Taking responsibility* for my physical and mental health is like using a tool. We use tools to fix, repair and build things. **#TakeResponsibility FixYourself #SelfRepair**

I don't blame my narcissist mother for who I am today. I actually thank her. FUCK, if I hadn't experienced the shit I've been through, I would not be qualified to write this book.

Crack on to the next chapter...

CHAPTER 10

Rebuild your own shit... Without anyone's concern about how you're going to improve your own life.

~ Sharon Lee Zapata

REBUILD YOUR OWN SHIT

[Plus + the top 10 list to do this]

Rebuild Your Shit... seems we are always in repair mode. Hard lessons learned and the changes we make so we don't go through the same shit over and over.

"I don't ever want to let you down." This is what I tell myself. I make it a habit of talking to myself as if I were talking to a good old friend. Think about it...
Nobody knows me better than me.
Nobody knows you better than you.

All your hidden secret thoughts, cheating strategies, agendas, and oh fuck! moments... If you are silent as you read this... Good. I want you to feel the silence. This is where the impact will be made. What impact?

The one that I'm slipping you… like a love note under the table as I write. I want you to be resilient. You see, so many of us are conditioned to be concerned with what others are going to *think* about us.

The commotion we all live in is thick with opinions, thoughts, yet nobody really goes home to 'think' about your ass or my ass… People are too wrapped up in their own heads; with their cable T.V., Netflix, Hulu, watching the news, useless videos on their phones, or watching makeover shows instead of giving their own personal lives a makeover…

We are not obliged to absorb the unhappiness of others just because they choose to spew it in our direction. There is great freedom in life that comes from remembering this.

Don't let any other damages consume you when you are seeking to re-build yourself up a new level. **#getshitdone** You and I do three things: BIRTH. LIVE. DIE. That sounds so dark, but it's a keeper [like they say down here in Texas… it's a keeper fucker]

When you're going to rebuild your life, your finances, your relationships, your whatever the hell needs to be rebuilt….

Remember the voices of our critics, the doubts... and even the fears that are implanted in us can only take on a life of their own if we allow it to happen. You exist for a reason and you better fucking realize how special you are before it's too late. Don't let anyone steal your creativity with their gloomy unconscious like energy.

I have had to 'rebuild my own shit' so many times in my life. As I write this book, I am going through it. I hope this book helps you as much as it is helping me... it's my optimal therapy instead of taking pills for an 'over creative mind'. I have so much physical and mental energy that sometimes I think something is wrong with me.

Is it too much coffee? No.

Is it too much exercising? No.

Is it too much _____ whatever? You fill in the blank in.

I have learned to embrace my crazy sometimes misdirected energy because one day I will be an old lady smoking her weed sitting under a tree with her flowers and a cold beer thinking, "I should've written that fucking little book: Middle Finger Happiness..."

My brain never stops thinking and telling me to write that 'thought' down. Most first-rate writers have this weird compulsion to write. They'll write in a journal, a diary, on loose leaf paper, on an app they downloaded to their phone... or their blog. So, yeah I am that weird enchanting person who carries tiny notebooks with me at all times or I send myself text messages. I can't remember every single idea... so I jot it down. This is how I am able to create so much content so easily.

You exist for a reason and you
better fucking realize how special
you are before it's too late. Don't
let anyone steal your creativity
with their gloomy unconscious
like energy.

- Sharon Lee Zapata

So, let's go to never-never-look-back-land while I give you my top 10 list on **#RebuildYourOwnShit**

TOP-10 List for Rebuilding Your Own Shit.

1. You are worthy of so much more. Do not doubt who you are.

2. Change requires getting fucking uncomfortable. When everything is predictable it becomes boring... and there is no growth

3. Embrace your mistakes... this is what makes you wiser and ready for the next chapter in your life.

4. Do not have any regrets for your choices... remember at one time it's something you fucking wanted

5. Learn something new... a language, technology, a skill, a musical instrument, etc...

6. Build real relationships with people who have your best interest... don't go after fake people who will just lick the flavor off your tootsie pop

7. You were born with factory-installed gifts and talents. Use them up... they were meant to be shared and worn out.

8. Remember, we all have an invisible expiration date stamped on us... We don't' get to say "When"

9. Learn to proceed quickly when opportunities present themselves... all opportunities have an expiration date.

10. Don't listen to those scary "what-if-this-doesn't-work" stomach churning moments. Don't' be afraid to fail.

CHAPTER 11

Sometimes you're not supposed
to be invited...
If you're being underestimated,
this just means you are
supposed to create your own
success.

~ Sharon Lee Zapata

MOVE THE PROBLEM

This is a tiny story I read in a tiny book:
'Think Like A Lawyer Don't' Act Like One'
written by Aernoud Bourdrez.

He has the best short story about moving a problem.

Sam's lying in bed, but he can't sleep.

Sarah asks him what's wrong.

"Tomorrow I have to pay Max $5,000 dollars, but I don't' have it."

"Is that it?" says Sarah.

She picks up the phone and calls Max.

"Hi Max," she says

"Listen, Sam was supposed to pay you tomorrow, but he doesn't have the money. Bye!" and hangs up.

"Now you can sleep and Max can't."

The reason I share this little story with you is because it simply shows us how we can over-think a solution to a problem we have. We have to be our own problem solvers. Don't bitch, complain or whine about how you can't do something... This does nothing to fix things. It only sucks up time and energy that could be used to repair or find a remedy.

When we are faced with a tough struggle or problem, we'll always discover:

- Who we really are

- What we're made of

CHAPTER 12

Be proud of your inability to fit in a category, be labeled or defined by the world...

~ Sharon Lee Zapata

3 WORDS THAT WILL GET YOU WHAT YOU WANT

This is originally from one of my blog post:
TheBitchyBusinessBriefs.com

In this world *[especially the social media world]* we live in… where a good writer is supposed to deliver messages about being positive and empowering it can be very sobering to know that *we all* go through *funk* times…

Today I'll admit that I am in a funk… not quite a depression, but just down about shit that's happening in my life.

The great news about this… I know it's temporary. I know this funk will pass and so will the dark black cloud… As humans, we all go through this shit.

What's even harder to accept, as a *'creative'* who wants to help others feel awesome is whether or not to share this with my audience? Being a creative is a blessing and a curse. I can't *turn off* my creativity. It's always on.

I say, fuck it… *"I will share this"* – because there is someone else out there who could read this and feel better about life, about their struggles or whatever other shit they're going through too.

I always say… life is a process; everything is a process AND process is messy. If there's anything I know for sure, most of us humans are actually turned-on or inspired when we see another person conquer their struggle or little demons…

Sometimes it can be hard to kick those little demons nipping at our heels. Kick 'em to the curb I say! …And stomp on 'em like ca-ca-roaches [hey, that's what my grandmother called them… and this has stuck with me since childhood. Damn ca-ca-roaches]

Let's get back to 3 Words that will get you what you want… or will get you on the path to what you want.

 [1.] PERCEIVE [meaning: to become aware] Take a moment to realize exactly what it is that you want. Not just kinda, sorta want. You have to know exactly what you want.

You know, that something that excites the crap outta you, makes your entire being come to life and feel amazing… this is your WHY. When you find your WHY – – it will drive you daily down the path of satisfaction, creativity, and you'll feel "whole" … not empty.

[2.] UNDERSTAND – We love to hear about a bad situation [*shituation*] where the ending was uber positive. That the person who was spiraling down picked themselves up and got out of their black hole. You gotta understand and get it in your gut that you can do it. If you don't think you can, then you may need to do some work on your self-image and your skills. Yes, both.

I'm not saying you have to look like those fancy photo-shopped people in the magazine. I'm saying be the best you that you can be. We are all born with factory installed gifts and talents. Somewhere down your messy road of life, you took the wrong turn and you quit working on *YOU*. Hey, if deep down in your gut you don't believe you can do it, either you need to dramatically improve the skills required to get there—which you can often do along the way—or your self-image needs a kick in the ass… Or you are committed to your self-doubt. Don't commit to self-doubt. Fuck that.

[3.] ACTION – Yes bitches you knew this was coming…
Take massive actions in the direction of what you want. From personal experience I know for sure that you will encounter hurdles, obstacles, and setbacks when you are taking 'actions' to your dreams, your goals, and that big ass project. Make that effort. Make the motion.

It is just part of the molding process of turning you into the person you need to be to experience what it is you want to achieve. These tests are an important part of the process. Like I always say, "Process is messy." So I hope these (3) three words will help you in your great adventure to your dreams. You may not know all the steps you need to take to get to your destination. No worries. It doesn't matter. Just figure out the first one. Take it. ...And be tenacious a motherfucker.

The path will reveal itself to you as you go. And like I mentioned, there will be little demons nipping at your heels like... self-doubt, fear, low self-image and other shit as you make your way to fulfilling your WHY. These nasty things will try to stand in your way at almost every step. Just stomp on them like ca-ca-roaches.

Crack on!

Photo by Gratisography

CHAPTER 13

You may not know all the steps you need to take to get to your destination. No worries. It does not matter. Just figure out the first one. Take it. ...And be tenacious as a motherfucker.

- Sharon Lee Zapata

WHO IS KEEPING YOU AT THE BOTTOM OF YOUR GAME?

We are the *gatekeeper* that keeps us away from our *next move... the next level up.* Even with tears in our eyes dammit, we have to dissolve that dirty black cloud that's dripping shit on us. You know who is keeping you at the bottom of your game? YOU.

You are getting in your own way.

Who says you have to hang on to heart-ache, drama, and other fuckery? Most people don't realize a decision is simply a choice that has results. We have to choose to let things go and move on.

Yes choice. No choice.

Yes choose. No choose.

None of this *I think... I might...*

Do it.

Don't do it.

Get results or don't get results.

Everything can come alive when you pump some firm decisions and put motion into place. Don't suffer in silence. Speak up when you are talking to yourself. Because there will be days when nobody is around to hear you.

It can be complicated to stand our ground when there is no ground to stand on. I've had days where I felt like an ice cube that shattered on the cement. Looking back at those moments, I realized if I couldn't be strong for me... then I couldn't be strong for others who were looking up to me.

Who is looking up to me? My two sons. If there is anything I can leave behind for my boys... it's self-worth, self-belief, confidence, kindness, leadership, and love.

Fireball-proficient people are the ones who move forward. They know it's up to them to create and even destroy in order to build their best life.

The word 'destroy' is a strong word.

The word 'create' is also a strong word.

I love these words.

They go hand in hand in the human landscape.

We all create and destroy.

CREATE: build, make, design, produce, establish

DESTROY: consume, smash, wipeout, damage

Nobody is going to knock on your door and make your life *'happen'*. Nobody is going to create your life... only you and your decisions and choices. Or your lack of decisions and your lack of choices..

Change the old rules inside your head. If things don't feel right.. then you need to change. Consider the actions of having to change your thinking like you change your underwear. SHIT thinking is not good for you... that's what could be keeping you at the bottom of your game.

Start off today... right now as you're reading this page to take yourself to a new level in your game.

When I was a single mom with my first son, I had an Image Consulting Business. I had that business for 13 years. It was a multi-level marketing opportunity that I found in the local newspaper. Yeah, this is old school bitches... 1994 when people would put ads in the newspaper to hire other people.

I treated this opportunity like a motherfucking job [not a soccer mom hobby]... I took it seriously. I presented Image Consulting workshops to Wells Fargo Bank corporate employees and other professional organizations. There were tough times when I didn't have enough sales for the month and I wasn't able to pay my electric bill. Fuck! ...And my 3rd grader at the time had to do his homework by candle light.

That night I promised myself *never again* would I be in that shitty position.

This is how I handled the current spot I was in. I told myself, "It was my fault that the electric bill did not get paid. It was my fault that I did not make enough sales that month to create the income I needed."

I didn't blame the economy.
I didn't blame my ex-husband.
I didn't blame the government.
I didn't blame the potential clients...

I took full blame and responsibility. I knew that I was responsible for keeping ME at the bottom of my game. That's how a strong-minded person thinks. I didn't need to put on my big-girl panties. Shit, I didn't need panties to change my circumstances. I needed a game-changing attitude.

Drops mic...

CHAPTER 14

Don't get mad.
Don't get even.
Just do better.
So much better...
Accelerate above.
Become so consumed in your
own success that you
forget it ever happened

- Sharon Lee Zapata

AUDACIOUS WORD VOMIT!

[one of my personal favorite chapters]

This audacious word vomit is brought to you by my 3rd cup of coffee and the music in my ear-buds. [listening to Dare by the Gorillaz] This audacious word vomit [or brain-dump] you're about to read is just for you sugar lips! Do you need some new moves in your business, in your life, or in your relationship(s)?

This is written in no particular order. I found this brain dump I wrote back in 2016... And now I choose to share it with you inside my book.

- Dealing with our personal reality is ALWAYS the answer;

- Expectations are NEVER the answer

- We live in a world of possibilities.

- We also live in a world that is so *information* dense

- Take what applies and leave the rest

- Your life rituals are the results of your growth... what are you doing daily?

- Your relationship rituals are the result of your relationship growth… or relationship death [goes, either way, sugar lips]

- We all want certainty and variety at the same time. I am laughing as I write that last sentence… no such thing.

- You can get certainty for a little while…then this will get fucking boring, hence the variety will not entice

- How do you stack your wins?

- How do you stack your losses?

- Don't expect small thinkers to 'teach' you anything big

-Make noise in your head… the kinda noise that is like a Super bowl audience cheering for their team to win!

- Just stand up inside yourself and blow that shit obstacle down!—make the Big Bad Wolf proud! *{you remember the story of Three Little Pigs?}*

Yeah, the big bad wolf would huff-and puff and blow those little pigs shitty tiny houses down… Until one smarty-pants pig built his house outta bricks… and fucked it all up for the big bad wolf!

- If you're not moving forward... everything is moving past you quickly.

-Find your own way... don't duplicate—don't copy

- Write your obituary while you're sipping on tequila... here is where the truth will come out...

-When writing, keep in mind that readers want to know you're just as fucked up as them... we connect-the-dots in our hearts like this.

-Don't leave yourself inside the shadows... Get out to the shiny as fuck areas!

Photo by Gratisography

-If you're a leader or influencer, remember, your audience is human like you. Teach them to use all the colors in the box [last time I checked even broken crayons still color...] Your audience also lives with hurt, passion, hope, and they want to wake up with purpose, love, and peace. Share your stories that you're embarrassed about - - that's how we help each other repair the broken parts of us.

P.S. When I say your audience... It's not just a social media audience. It could be your children, your friend(s), a total stranger... anyone you can influence in a positive way; with your stories of fuck-ups and hurt. *Connect-the-dots with our heart-strings.*

CHAPTER 15

For the play-it-safers
I am under no
obligation
to make sense to you

#OnlySmartMotherFuckers

- Sharon Lee Zapata

BRAVERY LIVES IN THE DARK CRACKS

[5-yrs. Old Sharon]

I've been alive long enough to know that we should live as if we have no limits with our gifts and our abilities. I've finally embraced my ever-changing gift of writing as one of my top abilities. It doesn't make me an expert. It simply helps me understand myself and others better.

**Becoming an expert is not an episode...
It's a process.
Experts don't have to convince.
They let people feel 'understood'
because they've been there.**

- Sharon Lee Zapata

I read somewhere... "What people are ashamed of usually makes a good story." This story is a good struggle story I spoke about this in an earlier chapter. At such a young age [5 or 6 years old] I had to deal with my little world... I'll briefly share it again. When I was in kindergarten, I would try to run away from home many weekends. Why the weekends? I just remember that my parents would be drinking and arguing all the fucking time on weekends... [*This will lead you to the next CHAPTER 16 THAT'S NOT MY NORMAL... THAT'S NOT YOUR NORMAL*]

So I would pack up my little suitcase. It had large beautiful bright orange and yellow daisies with big black polka-dots and a white background. I would pack all my coloring books and crayons and stuff animals inside this suitcase. I don't remember my parents ever trying to stop me from running away. Neither one of them would ever ask, "Hey, where do you think you're going?" I would just walk out the door... I remember hearing my narcissist mother laugh as I would open the front door and look back. Then I would sit outside under the stairwell of our apartment in Houston, TX.

Sitting there looking up at the night sky and poking at a dandelion flower with a little stick.

At this young age I realized that me and the little flower had bloomed in the dark in the crack of the sidewalk. This memory made an enormous impact on my life. Crazy... here I am writing about it many, many years later.

The dandelion didn't ask to be put there.

It simply bloomed in the dark... in the crack of the sidewalk.
It didn't look around and ask for permission.
It had no limiting potential... only purpose.
Its purpose was to distribute more tiny dandelion seeds so other dandelions could bloom too.

I am not ashamed of this story... finding bravery in the fucking cracks of life is the outcome from this memory. It's mighty powerful. I consider this one of my very first #MiddleFingerHappiness experiences.

I do realize there are much more devastating experiences other people have been through. At 5 or 6 years old, I didn't know there was an exit inside my head. I didn't know there was an entrance either... All I knew is there was stuff inside my head... and I didn't like it. When we are weakened we have to find our super hero strength. That's where we find a way to pull through. That's where fucking bravery lives...

Inside the cracks of sunlight and inside the cracks of darkness. It's only available a few hours of the day. The older I get... I see how bravery likes to hang out with a few four-letter words like: - Fuck & Hope -
"Fuck, I hope this works." - - Those words have been on my lips so many times... Like Sriracha Sauce on my scrambled

eggs. (Don't judge. This taste is extraordinary!) Whenever I've had to go through a difficult circumstance, make tough decisions, or when I've had to deal with my bouts of depression... I have whispered to myself, "Fuck, I hope this works."

Photo from Gratisography

CHAPTER 16

I am a little Wabi-Sabi
A Japanese term which means:
That which is perfect
because it's a little fucked up

- Sharon Lee Zapata

THAT'S NOT MY NORMAL
THAT'S NOT YOUR NORMAL

This chapter is originally from an article I wrote on
https://medium.com/@sharonleezapata
The original title was: What Fucking Parts of You to Let Go.

Since Middle Finger Happiness came into my head during the Thanksgiving – Christmas holidays [2017], I decided to re-purpose what I wrote and *re-name this Chapter: That's Not My Normal – That's Not Your Normal*. Because let's face it, none of us are *normal*. **#FreakBitches**

So, I took a rest and distanced myself from my work and my writing over the Labor Day weekend… This actually increased my creativity and it got me out of the vibration from a bad week I previously had. There is a progression to everyone and to everything that we are not aware of.

When you see someone with kick-ass experience… remember they had challenges and fuck-ups; they just didn't stop. They kept on messing up… and they kept on messing up. **#RinseAndRepeat**

They kept on looking for a new way when the old way didn't work. When you recognize you have a 'problem'…You no longer have a problem - - You have a recognition for a solution.

Our life can be predictable.
Our life can be unpredictable.
Some days we can be fulfilled and happy.
Some days we can be alone and lonely.

A little dirty secret I will share with you… the reason I've seen my endeavors, my writing and my projects improving is that I have found comfort in the chaos. It's NOT how many people read or follow me… it's that **ONE** person who I can help. Nothing is saturated… just create something that is kick-ass… something that can stand out.

The social kindness that I see with Social Media is simply the consistency to show up and inspire. Inspiration comes in so many forms. Telling a bad situation to fuck off is actually inspiring. Telling *yourself* not to be so fucking focused on *you* is the inspiration you may need to move forward today.

The person who embraces their communication to help others owns a special kind of freedom.

Their freedom is not worrying about who likes their art, their work, their writing, their profession...

Sometimes you have to experience someone else's voice until you find your own.

- Sharon Lee Zapata

A 'hinge-point' I see, is how people are not leading themselves... they wait for others to lead. You and I cannot cling on to who we used to be or what we used to do... Do not become attached to the older version of who you were [especially if it was a little fucked up version of who you were]. Hanging on to all the things you and I used to be...

120

will only keep us in stuck-mode. ***That's not my normal - -
That's not your normal.***

Learn how to capture those awesome ideas that pop into your exceptional brain… write shit down or text yourself. You cannot remember every amazing idea. I will leave you with this conception [because I am out of coffee]…

66

The understanding of love, fate, and regret is simply the warm sympathy and empathy for the frailty of the human landscape we live in. We can always be kinder and we can always not let people fuck with us too. Cheers! To YOUR Middle Finger Happiness.

CHAPTER 17

Sometimes you just have to chuck it in the fuck it bucket... And move on

- Sharon Lee Zapata

TICK. TOCK. YOUR LIFE IS NOT GOING TO WAIT FOR YOU

I will step forward with this last chapter. I will be judged... No biggie. I say, "Get in line."   There is a line of people who judge me and judge you. **#GetInLineBitches**

Your life is not going to wait for you. Every day, week, month, year... every season that comes and goes will not wait for you.   If you're feeling like a tiny midget is stabbing you in the foot to make some changes with your life... take action and DO IT.

What you did two or three or even ten years ago has brought you to where you are today. Hell, even what you did today... has brought you to this very moment. The first step you took to make a change was scary as fuck. You probably thought there were limits to taking those chances on yourself.
If you want *it* bad enough...
What do you know?
What do you *need* to know?

Explore the grounds you've never been to...
+
Step forward and be judged...

Don't avoid uncertainty... this is where the judgment will be. This is where the new level of who you are becoming will be. There is no instruction manual that comes attached to you and your life.

If we're ever going to do something bigger than ourselves, we will have to wage the wars inside our head. There are so many new levels to WHO YOU ARE. You will continue to experience love, joy, satisfaction, hurt, pain and shitty circumstances. You see, it's a combination of those ingredients that create your life. It's how you react to these ingredients that will be your life...

There will always be the next hurdle to overcome... Like the Whack-A-Mole game we play at Chuck-E-Cheese. Whacking those challenges with our grit and our **#NoFucksGiven** energy.

Since you've made it this far down the wormhole of this book, I'd like to say wouldn't it be great if your life did came with an owner's manual? [like the one in your glove compartment for your car]. The owner's manual would tell you how to handle every situation you go through in life. ...like turn to page 3 for a few words of safety. Your safety, and the safety of others is very important. And operating your life is an important responsibility. This manual would also come with a WARNING: Don't be committed to your doubt. **#GetShitDone**

You should know or at least have an idea of what's next in your space? Your life is not going to wait for you... What are you going to design? What art are you going to create? What project are you going to take on? What business are you going to start? What books are you going to write? What job are you going to go after? What part of your life needs improving? ...and the list goes on.

If you're ever in doubt it's simply because you're not fully committed to the process of your progress. Every day you live is an opportunity to embrace what's next in your space... Don't commit to your doubt.

If we're ever going to do something bigger than ourselves, we will have to wage the wars inside our head.

- Sharon Lee Zapata

The thought of how life is not going to wait for me didn't hit my radar until I realized I had waited too long to detach from many bull-shit situations.

So, why is it that we stick around and place ourselves in situations we know are going to cause us pain? I can't answer this question for you, however, I can answer it for "me". In my mind, I was waiting or hoping that the moments I invested in that situation would turn out the way I expected.

Lesson learned:
Don't assume anything…
View and recognize everything…
Go get your **#MiddleFingerHappiness** because your life is not going to wait for you.

Peace out,
Sharon Lee Zapata

Don't prove others wrong.
Prove yourself right...
At the end of the day,
ass-wipe people will always suck.
No time to prove anything to them

#HighHopesDontWaitBitch

- Sharon Lee Zapata

ABOUT THE AUTHOR

SHARON LEE ZAPATA

Photo: Brian Martin www. martinphoto.co.uk

Sharon owns all of her unbelievable successful mistakes and actions. From creating a company on a cocktail napkin , a podcast, writing three books in nine months, becoming the CEO of The Zapata Group, working in her art studio, and not giving up on herself in the darkest moments of her depression. These priceless uncertain actions have taught her to be a savvy opportunist. Sharon has learned to take all the bull shit she's experienced and turn it into something sharp and positive. Middle Finger Happiness is her favorite tattoo she has on her arm.

She is the recipient of the Latina Trendsetter Award from H.E.R.O. and the recipient of The Excellence Award from American Intercontinental University. Her speaking platforms range from women's conferences to colleges. She's learned to re-invent herself in order to take herself up another level. **#RinseAndRepeat**

With her bold misdirected energy, she is a hunter and gatherer of all her experiences she generously shares without attribution inside her signature small batch storytelling, speaking engagements, and Learnshops [workshops]. Sharon delivers her all when she attempts anything except for dusting her furniture... she doesn't give a fuck about dust. Sharon lives in Houston, Texas. She is married; has a younger son and a grown up son; two rescue pit-mix dogs and one ninja cat!

CONNECT

Email

info@thebitchybusinessbriefs.com

sharon@thezapatagroup.net

Website

SharonLeeZapata.com

Instagram: @SharonLeeZapata

Twitter: @SharonLeeZapata

Facebook: facebook.com/sharonleezapata

www.linkedin.com/in/sharonleezapata

LIST OF ALL THE HASH-TAGS USED IN THIS BOOK:

#MiddleFingerHappiness

#TheBitchyBusinessBriefs

#GetShitDone

#NoFucksGiven

#GetInLineBitches

#RinseAndRepeat

#DoNotFuckWithMe

#SecretTime

#FreakBitches

#RebuildYourOwnShit

#ThisIsMe

#BeenThereDoneThat

#FixYourself

#MovingOnMoments

#NoTimeForBullshit

#PeaceOut

#Shituation

#HulkSmash

#SecretTimeBitch

#Fucktard

#GetYourShitTogether

#PushYourself

#Boom #Bam #Bitch

#YouBeYou

#WeFeedHTX

LIST OF 66 Powerfully Positive Words

66 Powerfully Positive Words (in no particular order):

1. Fantastic
2. Stupendous
3. Fabulous
4. Magnificent
5. Good
6. Great
7. The best
8. Better than ever
9. Incredible
10. Unbelievable
11. Tremendous
12. Prodigious
13. Marvelous
14. Wonderful
15. Brilliant
16. Superb
17. Terrific
18. Excellent
19. Remarkable
20. Exceptional
21. Phenomenal
22. Extraordinary
23. Amazing
24. Awesome
25. Colossal
26. Brilliant
27. Stunning
28. Out of this world
29. Enormous
30. Splendid

31. Glorious
32. Superlative
33. Grand
34. Unmatched
35. Untouchable
36. Unbeatable
37. Best ever
38. Outstanding
39. Supreme
40. First-class
41. First-rate
42. Joyful
43. Delightful
44. Committed
45. Impressive
46. Boundless
47. Unlimited
48. Abundant
49. On top of the world
50. Astonishing
51. Mind-blowing

52. Mind-boggling
53. Sensational
54. Awe-inspiring
55. Spectacular
56. Radiant
57. Extreme
58. Especially
59. Particular
60. Staggering
61. Superb
62. Unparalleled
63. Unrivaled
64. Supreme
65. Invincible
66. Fucking Unbelievable

Made in the USA
Columbia, SC
28 March 2021